Daily Skill Builders:
General Science
Grades 5–8

By
WENDI SILVANO

COPYRIGHT © 2008 Mark Twain Media, Inc.

ISBN 978-1-58037-484-2

Printing No. CD-404103

Mark Twain Media, Inc., Publishers
Distributed by Carson-Dellosa Publishing LLC

Visit us at www.carsondellosa.com

Table of Contents

Table of Contents (cont.)

Introduction to the Teacher

Both the No Child Left Behind Act and standardized testing require students to meet certain proficiency standards. These Daily Skill Builders are designed to provide students with the opportunity to review or gain extra practice with the skills they are learning in their regular curriculum. They were written with the National Science Education Standards in mind. A matrix correlating the activities with the standards they address is included on page 1.

Suggestions for Use

Each activity page is divided into two reproducible sections that can be cut apart and used separately. Activities could be used in class as a warm-up, a review of a topic covered earlier in the year, as extra practice on a topic currently being studied, in a learning center for review or extra practice, or as a homework assignment.

Organization

Activities are arranged by topic, with the primary focus of this book being on the physical and earth sciences. A smaller life sciences section is also included. The table of contents identifies the skills that each activity covers. Since standardized testing is an important component of education, a few activities provide practice in standardized test-taking formats. This helps students become more familiar and comfortable with the format and provides test-taking practice.

At the back of the book (p. 83) is a copy of the Periodic Table of Elements, for use with activities 15, 17, and 25.

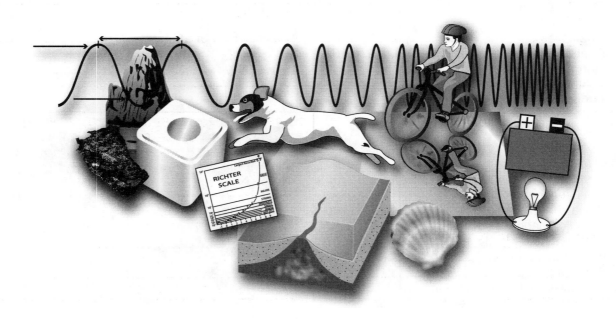

NSES Standards Matrix for Grades 5–8

Standard	Activities
Unifying Concepts and Processes	
Systems, order, and organization	15, 16, 25, 107, 128, 132, 134, 135, 143, 144, 145
Change, constancy, and measurement	5, 20, 23, 29, 38, 39, 44, 85, 86, 87, 88, 96, 99, 100, 125, 129, 130
Evolution and equilibrium	43, 96, 136
Form and function	8, 11, 46, 47, 75, 78, 79, 106, 116, 117
Science as Inquiry Standards	
Understanding about scientific inquiry	1, 2, 3, 4, 5, 103
Abilities necessary to do scientific inquiry	1, 3, 4, 5, 19, 39, 66, 68
Physical Science Standards	
Properties and changes of properties in matter	6, 7, 8, 9, 10, 11, 12, 13, 14, 15, 16, 17, 18, 19, 20, 21, 22, 23, 24, 25, 26, 27, 28, 29, 30, 31, 32
Motions and forces	35, 36, 37, 38, 40, 41, 42, 43, 44, 45, 46, 47, 48, 49, 50, 96, 97, 98, 99, 100, 102
Transfer of energy	29, 30, 31, 32, 33, 34, 48, 49, 50, 51, 52, 53, 54, 55, 56, 57, 58, 59, 60, 61, 62, 63, 64, 65, 66, 67, 68, 69, 70, 71, 72, 73, 74, 96, 97, 111, 112, 141
Life Science Standards	
Structure and function in living systems	139, 140, 141, 142, 143, 144, 145, 146, 147, 148, 149, 150, 151, 152, 153, 154, 155, 156, 157, 158, 159, 160, 161, 162
Diversity and adaptations of organisms	142, 143, 144, 145, 146, 147, 148, 149, 150, 151, 152, 153, 154, 155, 156, 157, 158, 159, 160, 161, 162
Earth and Space Science	
Structure of the earth system	75, 76, 77, 78, 79, 80, 81, 82, 83, 84, 85, 86, 87, 88, 89, 90, 91, 92, 93, 94, 95, 96, 97, 98, 99, 100, 101, 102, 103, 104, 105, 106, 107, 108, 109, 110, 111, 112, 113, 114, 115, 116, 117, 118, 119, 120, 121, 122, 123, 124, 125, 126, 127, 128, 129, 130
Earth in the solar system	131, 132, 133, 134, 135, 136, 137, 138
Science in Personal and Social Perspectives	
Populations, resources, and environments	91, 92, 97
Natural hazards	96, 103, 104, 121, 122, 123, 124

Scientific Methods

ACTIVITY 1   Which Scientist Is Which?

Name:_____

Date:_____

Match the scientist with what he/she studies.

1. _____ paleontologist
2. _____ entomologist
3. _____ astronomer
4. _____ metallurgist
5. _____ agronomist
6. _____ hydrologist
7. _____ archaeologist
8. _____ psychologist
9. _____ chemist
10. _____ physicist
11. _____ botanist
12. _____ zoologist
13. _____ geneticist
14. _____ geologist
15. _____ meteorologist

a. metals
b. human behavior
c. insects
d. energy and force
e. water
f. plants
g. animals
h. prehistoric forms of life
i. rocks
j. structure and matter
k. soil and crop raising
l. weather
m. stars and planets
n. human DNA
o. past cultures

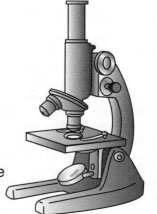

ACTIVITY 2   Branches of Science

Name:_____

Date:_____

Write the branch of science each of the fields below would belong to: **Physical Science, Earth and Space Science, Life Science, Mathematics, Social Science.**

1. Zoology _____
2. Astronomy _____
3. Physics _____
4. Anatomy _____
5. Anthropology _____
6. Geometry _____
7. Botany _____
8. Mineralogy _____
9. Meteorology _____
10. Chemistry _____

11. Statistics _____
12. Biology _____
13. Geology _____
14. Psychology _____
15. Seismology _____
16. Entomology _____
17. Archaeology _____
18. Logic _____
19. Genetics _____
20. Ornithology _____

Earth and Space Sciences

ACTIVITY 83 Weathering

Name:_____

Date:_____

Use the words in the box to fill in the blanks.

chemical	weathering	environment	characteristics
oxidation	mechanical	sediment	

Weathering is the process where conditions in the _____ break rocks

down into smaller pieces called _____. There are two kinds of weathering.

_____ weathering breaks rocks apart without

making changes to their _____ composition.

Each smaller piece maintains the same _____

as the bigger rock. Chemical _____ occurs

when the chemical composition of the rock is changed from water,

acids, _____, or other means.

ACTIVITY 84 Soil

Name:_____

Date:_____

Weathering breaks rocks into tiny fragments, but in order
to become soil, plants and animals must live in them. Unscramble the names of these things of
which soil is a mixture (not all will be in all soils.)

1. S L A V E E   _____
2. G W T I S   _____
3. S N T I E C S   _____
4. T R W E A   _____
5. C R K O   _____
6. R A I   _____
7. S L M N I E R A   _____
8. W R M S O   _____
9. G A L E A   _____
10. G F N U I   _____

Earth and Space Sciences

ACTIVITY 85   Gravitational Erosion

Name: _____

Date: _____

Erosion is the process that wears down sediments. It then transports them to new places where deposition occurs (or those bits of sediment that were worn away and moved are deposited). Match these types of gravitational erosion to their definitions.

slump	creep
rockslide	mudflows
mass movement	

1. When strong rock or sediment sits upon weaker materials, the pressure becomes too much to bear, and the sediment slips downslope in one large mass. _____

2. When large chunks of rock break loose and tumble downward, crashing into more rocks and setting them into motion also. _____

3. When gravity causes materials to slide downslope (fast or slow). _____

4. When heavy rains mix with dry sediment and the weight of the wet sediment causes it to slide downslope. _____

5. When sediments slowly inch their way down a slope due to gravity. _____

ACTIVITY 86   Glacial Erosion

Name: _____

Date: _____

Write "T" for true or "F" for false on each of these statements about glacial erosion.

1. _____ Glaciers begin to move because their weight becomes so great that it causes partial melting of snow and ice on the bottom of the mass.

2. _____ Glaciers slide quickly down a slope.

3. _____ As they move, glaciers carry debris from the surrounding area downslope.

4. _____ Striations or grooves on rock would indicate glacial movement.

5. _____ *Plucking* occurs as glaciers tear off leaves of surrounding trees as they move.

6. _____ The mixture of different sediments dropped by a glacier as it moves is called *till*.

7. _____ A moraine is a ridge of material deposited at the end of a glacier.

Earth and Space Sciences

ACTIVITY 87   Wind Erosion

Name:_____

Date:_____

Solve the crossword puzzle using the clues below.

ACROSS
3. Fine-grained particles tightly packed by wind
4. When rocks are pitted or polished by windblown sediments
5. Plantings of vegetation to slow wind erosion
6. When windblown sediments settle behind an obstacle, these are created.

DOWN
1. Wind eroding only fine-grained sediment, leaving behind coarse sediments
2. The part of vegetation that helps hold soil together

ACTIVITY 88   Water Erosion

Name:_____

Date:_____

Match these terms to their definitions:

rill erosion	gully erosion
sheet erosion	stream erosion

1. When water moving through a stream picks up and moves lightweight sediments and rolls heavier sediments, thus cutting a wider and deeper channel _____

2. When a tiny stream forms during rainfall, carrying away some soil and plants and leaving a scar _____

3. When rainwater covers a flat area until it is deep enough that it begins moving down a gentle slope, carrying sediments as it moves _____

4. When rainwater carves a broad, deep gash in the land as it moves large amounts of soil

_____

Earth and Space Sciences

ACTIVITY 89 **Groundwater and the Water Table**

Name:_____

Date:_____

1. What is meant by groundwater? _____

_____

2. What is the difference between permeable and impermeable rock? _____

_____

3. What is an aquifer? _____

_____

4. What is the water table? _____

_____

ACTIVITY 90 **Geysers, Caves, and Sinkholes**

Name:_____

Date:_____

Circle the correct word from the pair in the parentheses to make the statement true.

1. A geyser erupts when groundwater is (heated / increased)

   causing it to expand and forcing some of it up to the surface.

2. What shoots out of a geyser is (smoke / steam).

3. Caves are formed when groundwater dissolves

   (sandstone / limestone).

4. Stalactites hanging in caves are deposits of (slime / calcite)

   from dripping water.

5. If rock on top of a cave is (dissolved / fractured), a sinkhole may form.

Earth and Space Sciences

ACTIVITY 91 Energy Resources

Name:_____

Date:_____

List each of these resources under the correct column to indicate which are renewable resources and which are nonrenewable.

natural gas	wind	oil	solar energy
coal	hydroelectric power		geothermal energy

Renewable resources

1. _____
2. _____
3. _____
4. _____

Nonrenewable resources

1. _____
2. _____
3. _____

ACTIVITY 92 Earth's Materials and Resources Review/Test Practice

Name:_____

Date:_____

Shade in the circle for the correct answer.

1. Luster and hardness are two characteristics of _____.
   (a.) rocks   (b.) minerals   (c.) phosphates

2. One way minerals form is through the cooling of _____.
   (a.) magma   (b.) sediments   (c.) the atmosphere

3. Which types of rocks are formed because of changes in pressure and temperature?
   (a.) sedimentary   (b.) igneous   (c.) metamorphic

4. What is the process that breaks rocks into smaller and smaller pieces?
   (a.) compaction   (b.) abrasion   (c.) weathering

5. Which type of erosion are mudflows and rockslides?
   (a.) gravitational   (b.) glacial   (c.) water

6. In an aquifer, the rock is _____.
   (a.) impermeable   (b.) permeable   (c.) petrified

Earth and Space Sciences

ACTIVITY 93 **Composition of Oceans**

Name:_____

Date:_____

Salinity is a measure of the amount of salt dissolved in a substance. The Earth's oceans have a salinity of about 3.5%. There are a variety of dissolved salts in the ocean. Use the clues to help you place the names of these ocean salts in the correct place on the circle graph.

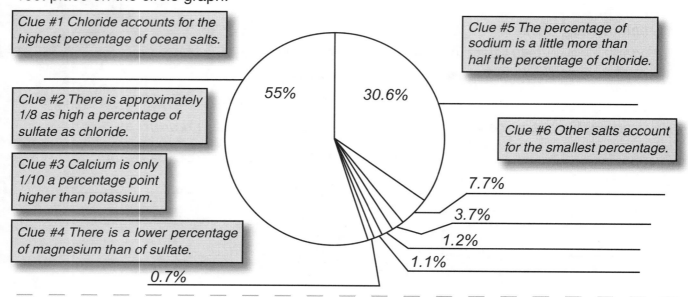

Clue #1 Chloride accounts for the highest percentage of ocean salts.

Clue #2 There is approximately 1/8 as high a percentage of sulfate as chloride.

Clue #3 Calcium is only 1/10 a percentage point higher than potassium.

Clue #4 There is a lower percentage of magnesium than of sulfate.

Clue #5 The percentage of sodium is a little more than half the percentage of chloride.

Clue #6 Other salts account for the smallest percentage.

55% 30.6%

7.7%

3.7%

1.2%

1.1%

0.7%

ACTIVITY 94 **Ocean Waves and Tides**

Name:_____

Date:_____

Use the words in the box to fill in the blanks.

moon	energy	crest	wind
trough	gravity	tides	particles

Ocean waves are rhythmic movements that carry _____ forward, even as the water _____ remain in place. The high point of a wave is called the _____, and the low point is called a _____. What causes the majority of ocean waves is _____.

_____, on the other hand, are not caused by winds, but rather by the interaction of _____ between Earth and the _____.

Earth and Space Sciences

ACTIVITY 95   Sea Floor

Name: _____

Date: _____

Match these features of the sea floor with their definitions.

1. _____ continental shelf
2. _____ continental slope
3. _____ abyssal plains
4. _____ mid-ocean ridge
5. _____ ocean trench

a. flat seafloor areas

b. deep, narrow trough in ocean

c. edge of continent that gradually slopes under the ocean

d. steep edge of continental shelf that slopes to the ocean floor

e. chain of mountains under the ocean

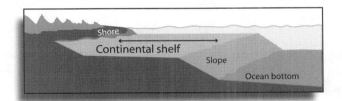

ACTIVITY 96   Earthquake Forces

Name: _____

Date: _____

The earth's crust and upper mantle are made up of a number of different segments called plates. Where these plates meet, they exert different kinds of pressure on each other. Sometimes the pressure becomes so great that the rock breaks and an earthquake occurs. Write the name of the type of stress or pressure defined in each statement.

| compression | tension | shear |

1. A force that stretches rock and makes it longer.

_____

2. A force that squeezes rock. _____

3. A force that causes rocks on both sides of a fault to slide past each other. _____

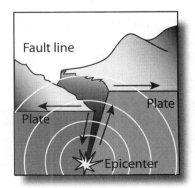

Earth and Space Sciences

ACTIVITY 97 Earthquakes

Name:_____

Date:_____

Solve the crossword puzzle using the clues below.

ACROSS

1. The point inside the earth where the energy release occurs
5. Surface point directly above an earthquake's focus
6. Seismic waves that cause rocks to move in the same direction as the waves

DOWN

2. Seismic waves that cause rock particles to vibrate at right angles to the direction of the waves
3. Waves produced by an earthquake
4. Seismic waves that reach Earth's surface and travel outward

ACTIVITY 98 Measuring Earthquakes

Name:_____

Date:_____

Use the words from the box to fill in the blanks.

seismograph	magnitude
Richter	energy
seismologists	seismic

Scientists who study earthquakes are called _____. They can

measure the _____ of an earthquake using an instrument called a

_____. A scale called the _____ scale describes the

amount of _____ released by an earthquake. Its measurements are

based on _____ waves that travel through the ground.

Earth and Space Sciences

ACTIVITY 99 Pangaea and Continental Drift

Name: _____

Date: _____

1. What is Pangaea? _____

    _____

    _____

    _____

2. What is the hypothesis of continental drift? _____

    _____

    _____

    _____

    _____

ACTIVITY 100 Sea Floor Spreading

Name: _____

Date: _____

Use the words from the box to fill in the blanks.

continuously	erupts	mid-ocean	molten
sea floor	older	spreading	

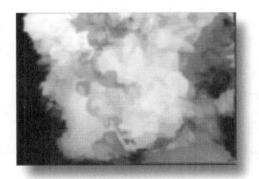

The theory of sea floor _____

says that _____ material beneath

the crust at the _____ ridge is

forced upward. It _____ and flows

downward, spreading out as it goes. This material

pushes _____ rock to both sides of

the ridge. This process _____ adds

material to the _____.

Earth and Space Sciences

ACTIVITY 101 **Plate Tectonics**   Name:_____

Date:_____

Unscramble the names of Earth's major lithospheric plates.

1. R S N E U A A I   _____

2. T N R C A C T I A   _____

3. F C A I P C I   _____

4. Z A C A N   _____

5. B R C A I E N A B   _____

6. F C N A I R A   _____

7. R N O T H E R A C I M N A   _____

8. T S U H O M R N A C I E A   _____

9. N D O I S T R A N A U A I L   _____

ACTIVITY 102 **Plate Boundaries**   Name:_____

Date:_____

Answer the questions with words from the box.
Words will be used more than once.

> transform boundary
> divergent boundary
> convergent boundary

1. Which type of boundary is the place where two plates move apart? _____

2. Which type of boundary is the place where two plates come together? _____

3. Which type of boundary is where two plates move in opposite directions as they slip past each other? _____

4. At which type of boundary is crust neither created nor destroyed?

   _____

5. Which type of boundary occurs mostly at the mid-ocean ridge?

   _____

Mid-ocean ridge

6. Which type of boundary is where the process of subduction sometimes occurs? _____

Earth and Space Sciences

ACTIVITY 103 Ring of Fire

Name: _____

Date: _____

Look at the map of the plate boundaries and the Earth's active volcanoes. What patterns can you see?

_____

_____

_____

_____

_____

_____

_____

_____

_____

_____

_____

ACTIVITY 104 Parts of a Volcano

Name: _____

Date: _____

Place these labels in the correct spot on the diagram of a volcano.

side vent	lava	vent	crater
magma	magma chamber	pipe	

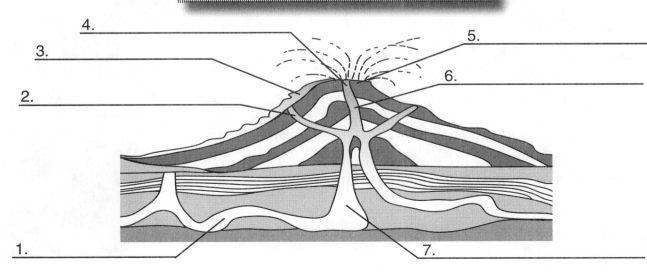

Earth and Space Sciences

ACTIVITY 105   Volcanoes

Name:_____

Date:_____

Write "T" for true or "F" for false.

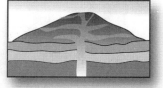

1. _____ *Magma* is melted rock within the earth.

2. _____ Once magma is exposed at the surface of a volcano, it is called lava.

3. _____ Cinder cone volcanoes are dome-shaped.

4. _____ Composite volcanoes have alternating layers of lava and rock.

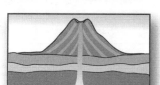

5. _____ Water vapor inside magma increases its explosive-ness.

6. _____ Silica-rich magma produces quiet, nonexplosive erup-tions.

7. _____ Shield volcanoes pour out lava in flat layers.

8. _____ *Tephra* is bits of rock and lava thrown from volcanoes.

ACTIVITY 106   Igneous Rock Features

Name:_____

Date:_____

Match each rock formation with its description.

a. batholiths	b. caldera	c. dikes
d. volcanic neck	e. sills	f. dome mountains

1. _____ These form when magma squeezes into vertical cracks.

2. _____ These form when magma squeezes between layers of rock.

3. _____ This forms when the top of a volcano collapses.

4. _____ Large rock bodies that form when magma cools under-ground

5. _____ The core of a volcano, left when it stops erupting and outer layers erode

6. _____ These form when horizontal layers of rock block rising magma.

Earth and Space Sciences

ACTIVITY 107 The Atmosphere

Name:_____

Date:_____

Next to each item below write which layer of the atmosphere it refers to.

1. Has most of Earth's weather   _____

2. Most planes fly in this layer.   _____

3. Most meteoroids break up in this layer.   _____

4. Reflects radio waves back to Earth   _____

5. Contains the coldest temperatures   _____

6. Contains electronically charged particles   _____

7. Has the ozone layer   _____

8. Has two parts   _____

9. Is the outermost layer   _____

10. We live here.   _____

ACTIVITY 108 Composition of the Atmosphere

Name:_____

Date:_____

Fill in the missing letters.

1. The atmosphere is 78% this gas: n __ __ r __ __ __ __.

2. The atmosphere is 21% this gas: __ __ y g __ __
    (which includes a form with three atoms bonded together,
    called o z __ __ __).

3. The remaining 1% is mostly a __ g __ __ and c __ __ b __ __
    __ i __ x __ __ __.

4. Besides these gases, the atmosphere contains w __ __ __ r v __ p __ __.

5. It also contains tiny solid and liquid particles of d __ __ t, s m __ __ __, s __ l __,
    and other c h __ __ __ c __ l __.

Earth and Space Sciences

ACTIVITY 109) Air Pressure

Name:_____

Date:_____

Write "T" for true or "F" for false.

1. _____ Air pressure is affected by the amount of air above an area and temperature.

2. _____ Warm air weighs more than cold air.

3. _____ The particles in cold air are more tightly packed than those in hot air.

4. _____ Air pressure is greater at the equator than at the north pole.

5. _____ Falling air pressure usually indicates that the weather is clearing.

6. _____ Air pressure is measured with a thermometer.

7. _____ Air pressure decreases as altitude increases.

8. _____ The barometer was invented by Albert Einstein.

ACTIVITY 110) Energy in the Atmosphere

Name:_____

Date:_____

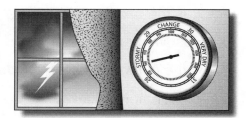

1. What is the source of most of the energy in Earth's atmosphere? _____

_____

2. This energy travels to Earth as what type of waves?

_____

_____

3. This energy reaches the Earth in the form of visible light and what two types of radiation?

_____

4. The reflection of sunlight in all directions is called what? _____

_____

5. When the heat that is usually radiated back into the atmosphere as infrared radiation gets trapped and forms a dome that holds heat in, this is called the _____ effect.

Earth and Space Sciences

ACTIVITY 111   Heat Transfer

Name:_____

Date:_____

Circle the word in each pair in the parentheses to make each statement correct.

1. The direct transfer of heat from one substance to another that it is touching is called (convection / conduction).

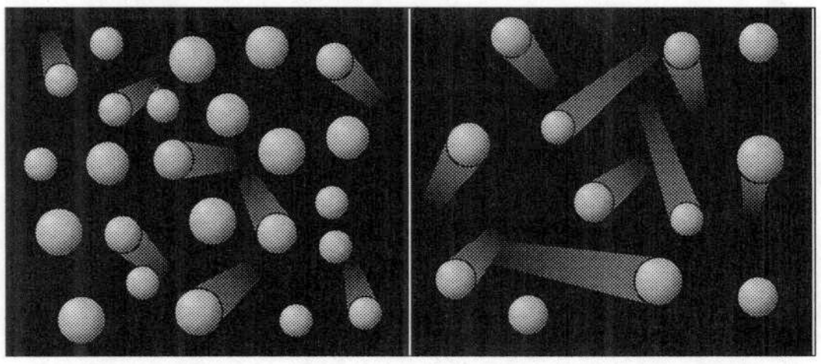

2. The (closer together / farther apart) the molecules are in a substance, the more effective they are at conduction heat.

3. (Conduction / Convection) is the transfer of heat by the flow of a heated material.

4. (Conduction / Convection) causes most of the heating of the troposphere.

5. Cooler air (sinks / rises), while warmer air (sinks / rises), causing air movement.

ACTIVITY 112   Winds

Name:_____

Date:_____

Rearrange the words in each row to make a sentence about winds.

1. occur cool meets air Winds when air warm

2. pressure Surface are winds caused differences by in air

3. atmosphere in Unequal causes the heating pressure differences air in

4. anemometer used measure An is wind to speed.

5. Narrow altitudes streams are of jet winds high belts strong at called

Earth and Space Sciences

ACTIVITY 113 The Coriolis Effect

Name:_____

Date:_____

Use the words in the box to fill in the blanks.

spinning	Coriolis	tropical	patterns
shifted	opposite	energy	polar

Solar _____ strikes the equator more directly. The warmer

_____ air tends to flow towards the colder poles, and _____

air tends to sink towards the equator. But the _____ of the earth has an

effect on this air movement. As the earth spins, winds are _____ and flow

on an angle. Those in the northern hemisphere blow _____

to those in the southern hemisphere. This effect is called the

_____ Effect. It results in certain, specific wind

_____ on Earth.

ACTIVITY 114 Global Winds

Name:_____

Date:_____

Use these terms to label the diagram of Earth's global winds.

Prevailing Westerlies (use 2x)	Polar Easterlies (use 2x)	
Northeast Trade Winds	Southeast Trade Winds	Doldrums

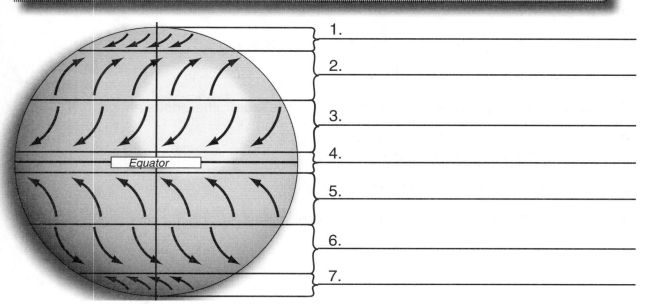

1. _____

2. _____

3. _____

4. _____

5. _____

6. _____

7. _____

Equator

Earth and Space Sciences

ACTIVITY 115 **Water in the Atmosphere**

Name:_____

Date:_____

Match the terms with their descriptions.

1. _____ humidity
2. _____ evaporation
3. _____ relative humidity
4. _____ dew point
5. _____ precipitation
6. _____ condensation
7. _____ dew

a. water condensed on a cold surface

b. any form of water falling from clouds

c. water vapor in the air becoming liquid

d. process by which water enters atmosphere

e. amount of water vapor in the air

f. temperature at which condensation begins

g. percentage of water vapor in the air compared to maximum possible

ACTIVITY 116 **Cloud Formation**

Name:_____

Date:_____

Number these steps in order to describe the process of cloud formation.

a. _____ Rising air expands and becomes cooler.

b. _____ Water vapor condenses onto particles in the air.

c. _____ Water enters the atmosphere through evaporation.

d. _____ Clouds form.

e. _____ Air is warmed near the ground, becomes less dense, and rises.

f. _____ The cooled air reaches its dew point.

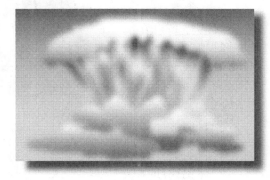

Earth and Space Sciences

ACTIVITY 117   Types of Clouds

Name:_____

Date:_____

Match the clouds to their description.

1. Which types of clouds form in flat layers and often bring drizzling rain or snow?

   _____

2. Which types of clouds are fluffy, heap-like clouds and usually indicate fair weather?

   _____

3. Which types of clouds are wispy and feathery and are made mostly of ice crystals?

   _____

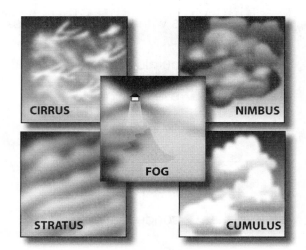

4. Any cloud that produces precipitation is called what? _____

5. What is a cloud forming at ground level called? _____

ACTIVITY 118   Precipitation

Name:_____

Date:_____

What does the word **precipitation** mean? _____

_____

Match these types of precipitation with their descriptions.

1. _____ rain

2. _____ sleet

3. _____ hail

4. _____ snow

5. _____ freezing rain

6. _____ drizzle

a. water vapor turning directly to ice crystals

b. raindrops that freeze as they fall

c. drops of water at least 0.5 mL in diameter

d. round pellets of ice

e. drops of water smaller than 0.5 mL

f. raindrops that freeze when they touch a cold surface

Earth and Space Sciences

ACTIVITY 119 Air Masses

Name: _____

Date: _____

Use the words in the box to fill in the blanks.

> tropical   polar   maritime   continental

1. What type of air mass forms over land and is dry?

   _____

2. What type of air mass forms over oceans and is humid?

   _____

3. What type of air mass forms over the tropics and is warm? _____

4. What type of air mass forms north or south of the 50 degree latitudes and is cold?

   _____

ACTIVITY 120 Fronts

Name: _____

Date: _____

For each description, tell which type of front occurs and what type of weather it brings.

1. When a fast-moving cold air mass meets a slow-moving warm air mass.

   Front type: _____

   Weather type: _____

2. When a faster-moving warm air mass collides with a slower-moving cold air mass.

   Front type: _____

   Weather type: _____

3. When a warm and a cold air mass meet, but neither has the force to move the other.

   Front type: _____

   Weather type: _____

4. When a warm air mass is stuck between two cool air masses

   Front type: _____

   Weather type: _____

Earth and Space Sciences

ACTIVITY 121   Storms

Name:_____

Date:_____

1. I often form in cumulonimbus clouds.
   I form when warm air rises rapidly and cools.
   I bring heavy rain and sometimes hail.
   What storm am I? _____

2. I form over warm water and get my energy from the humid, warm air of the ocean.
   My winds spiral inward toward areas of low pressure.
   I might last a week, until I run into land.
   What storm am I? _____

3. I form when warm air is drawn in at the base of a super-cell cloud and moves upward in powerful air currents.
   I reach down to touch the Earth's surface.
   I spin at speeds up to 450 km per hour.
   What storm am I? _____

ACTIVITY 122   Lightning

Name:_____

Date:_____

Write "T" for true or "F" for false.

1. _____ Lightning is the sudden discharge of both positive and negative electrical charges.

2. _____ Sheet lightning travels from cloud to cloud.

3. _____ Lightning heats the atmosphere to 54,000 degrees Fahrenheit.

4. _____ Lightning is always white.

5. _____ Lightning kills about 100 people per year in the U.S.A.

6. _____ Thunder results from the rapid cooling of the air around a lightning bolt.

7. _____ It is safe to be under a tree in a lightning storm.

8. _____ You should avoid touching metal objects during a lightning storm.

Earth and Space Sciences

ACTIVITY 123 Tornadoes

Name:_____

Date:_____

Circle the word in the parentheses that makes each sentence correct.

1. Most tornadoes move along a (front / coast).
2. They usually move from southwest to (northeast / northwest).
3. Most tornadoes last a few (hours / minutes).
4. The area of the United States where tornadoes are more common than anywhere else in the world is called Tornado (Lane / Alley).
5. Waterspouts spin more slowly than tornadoes because water is (heavier / warmer) than air.
6. Tornadoes can be detected with (funnel / Doppler) radar.

ACTIVITY 124 Hurricanes

Name:_____

Date:_____

Over which ocean does each of the following storms occur?

1. Hurricanes _____
2. Typhoons _____
3. Cyclones _____

Number the steps in order to describe how a hurricane forms.

a. _____ Wind speed increases until the storm reaches land.

b. _____ Air is continuously drawn into the system.

c. _____ Winds spiral inward toward the area of low pressure.

d. _____ Humid, warm air rises and forms clouds.

Earth and Space Sciences

ACTIVITY 125 **Predicting the Weather** Name:_____

Date:_____

1. What three things do weather balloons measure?

_____   _____   _____

2. List three sources from which meteorologists collect weather data.

_____   _____   _____

Match each of these instruments with what they measure.

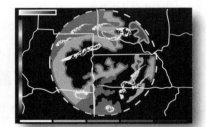

3. _____ wind vane   a. temperature

4. _____ barometer   b. relative humidity

5. _____ thermometer   c. wind direction

6. _____ anemometer   d. air pressure

7. _____ psychrometer   e. wind speed

- -

ACTIVITY 126 **Weather Maps** Name:_____

Date:_____

1. Name three things that might be indicated on a weather map.

_____   _____

_____

Which type of front does each symbol represent?

2. _____   3. _____

4. _____   5. _____

What does each symbol represent?

6. ≡ _____   7. △ _____   8. ● _____

9. ✳ _____   10. ◬ _____

Earth and Space Sciences

ACTIVITY 127　Climate

Name:_____

Date:_____

Climate is the average pattern of weather in an area over long periods of time. The earth has three main climate zones (polar, temperate, and tropical). Using the map of those zones, list in which zones each of the continents are located.

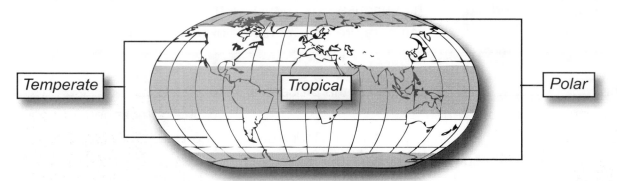

1. North America _____
2. South America _____
3. Africa _____
4. Asia _____
5. Australia _____
6. Europe _____
7. Antarctica _____

ACTIVITY 128　Climate Regions and Types

Name:_____

Date:_____

Next to each climate type, list the climate region it falls under.

1. Ice cap _____
2. Tundra _____
3. Arid _____
4. Mediterranean _____
5. Semiarid _____
6. Subarctic _____
7. Tropical wet _____
8. Humid subtropical _____
9. Tropical wet and dry _____
10. Marine west coast _____
11. Humid continental _____

Climate Regions

tropical

dry

polar

temperate marine

temperate continental

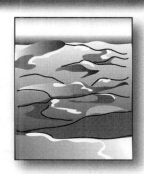

Earth and Space Sciences

ACTIVITY 129 The Greenhouse Effect and Global Warming

Name:_____

Date:_____

Use the words in the box to fill in the blanks.

gases	surface	greenhouse	global warming	increase
heating	prevents	temperatures	carbon dioxide	sun

The _____ effect is the process of natural _____ of the earth that occurs when _____ in the atmosphere, such as _____, trap heat. Radiation from the _____ passes through our atmosphere and heats the _____ of the earth. The greenhouse gases form a ceiling that _____ the heat and radiation from escaping back out of the atmosphere. _____ is a theory that says that Earth's average _____ are rising, partly because of an _____ in greenhouse gases.

ACTIVITY 130 Climatic Change

Name:_____

Date:_____

Explain how each of the events below could change the climate of a region or the entire world.

1. A huge volcanic eruption: _____
_____
_____
_____

2. Movement of the continents: _____
_____
_____

3. A change in the sun's energy output: _____
_____
_____

Earth and Space Sciences

ACTIVITY 131   The Earth and the Moon

Name: _____

Date: _____

1. What is caused by the: rotation of Earth? _____

   tilting axis of Earth and its revolution around the sun? _____

2. Where is the sun when there is an equinox, and how do the number of daylight and night-time hours compare at that time? _____

   _____

3. What causes changes in the moon's appearance? _____

   _____

   _____

4. Explain why the moon shines. _____

   _____

   _____

ACTIVITY 132   Phases of the Moon

Name: _____

Date: _____

Label each phase of the moon with the correct title.

New moon

Full moon

First quarter

Third quarter

Waxing gibbous

Waning gibbous

Waxing crescent

Waning crescent

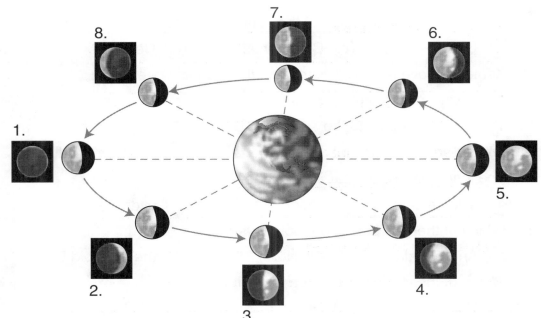

Earth and Space Science

ACTIVITY 133 Eclipses

Name:_____

Date:_____

Write "T" for true or "F" for false.

1. _____ Eclipses are caused by the revolution of the moon.
2. _____ Eclipses happen once a month.
3. _____ A solar eclipse occurs when the moon moves between the sun and the earth and casts a shadow on the earth.
4. _____ The darkest portion of the moon's shadow is called the umbra.
5. _____ A lunar eclipse occurs when the moon moves through the shadow of the Earth.
6. _____ All eclipses occur during full moons.
7. _____ All lunar eclipses are total eclipses.
8. _____ The outer part of the moon's shadow is called the penumbra.
9. _____ Total eclipses can be seen from anywhere on the earth.
10. _____ Solar eclipses last 6–10 hours.

ACTIVITY 134 The Solar System/ Test Practice

Name:_____

Date:_____

Shade in the circle of the correct answer.

1. The "sun-centered" model of the solar system was developed by _____.
   - (a.) Galileo
   - (b.) Copernicus
   - (c.) Newton

2. Kepler discovered that the orbits of the planets were _____.
   - (a.) always changing
   - (b.) circular
   - (c.) elliptical

3. The planets closest to the sun travel _____ than those farther away.
   - (a.) faster
   - (b.) slower
   - (c.) more erratically

4. The inner planets are _____ planets.
   - (a.) solid, rocky
   - (b.) gaseous
   - (c.) hydrogen

5. Which of these is part of our solar system?
   - (a.) Andromeda
   - (b.) the North Star
   - (c.) the Asteroid Belt

6. Which of these is NOT a moon of Jupiter?
   - (a.) Charon
   - (b.) Ganymede
   - (c.) Callisto

Earth and Space Sciences

ACTIVITY 135 Other Solar System Objects

Name:_____

Date:_____

Solve the crossword puzzle using the clues below.

ACROSS

1. The glowing cloud of gases surrounding a comet's nucleus
3. A comet's tails always point ____ from the sun.
6. A meteor that strikes Earth's surface
8. A possible icy cloud surrounding the solar system from which some comets originate
9. A comet has two or these—a dust one and an ion one.

DOWN

2. Small chunk of rock moving through space
4. A large chunk of rock traveling in space
5. Large chunk of ice, dust, rock fragments, or frozen gases that moves through space
7. What a meteoroid is called once it enters Earth's atmosphere

ACTIVITY 136 Stars

Name:_____

Date:_____

1. Write these colors of stars in order from hottest to least hot: yellow stars, bluish-white stars, reddish-orange stars.

   _____ (hottest) _____ (medium) _____ (least hot)

Write "T" for true or "F" for false.

2. _____ White dwarfs are stars that are near the end of their evolution.

3. _____ Our sun is a supergiant.

4. _____ When the outer portion of a star explodes, it produces a supernova.

5. _____ A neutron star contains electrons and neutrons.

6. _____ Nothing can escape the gravity field of a black hole.

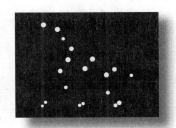

7. What is a nebula? _____

_____

Earth and Space Sciences

ACTIVITY 137   The Sun

Name:_____

Date:_____

1.   Label the parts of the sun using the terms in the box.

a._____
b._____
c._____
d._____
e._____
f._____

corona	chromosphere	photosphere
sunspot	prominence	core

2.   Which is the largest layer of the sun's atmosphere? _____
3.   Which layer of the sun's atmosphere is also called the surface? _____
4.   Where in the sun is energy produced by fusion? _____
5.   Which features on the sun look dark because they are slightly cooler than the rest of the sun? _____
6.   Which features are arching columns that blast material into space? _____

ACTIVITY 138   Galaxies

Name:_____

Date:_____

Use the words from the box to fill in the blanks.

enormous	spiral	Milky Way
irregular	shapes	gravitational
elliptical	core	stars

A galaxy is a large group of _____, dust, and gases that hold together because of their _____ pull on one another. There are three principal types of galaxies. _____ galaxies have spiral arms that wind outward from a central _____. Our galaxy, the _____, is this type. _____ galaxies are the most common type of galaxy. They are shaped sort of like footballs. Some are _____, and others are relatively small. _____ galaxies have a variety of _____ and sizes and are less common than the other types.

Life Sciences

ACTIVITY 139   Animal and Plant Cells

Name:_____

Date:_____

Use the descriptions of these cell parts to help you decide what the scrambled names are.

1. Controls what materials go in and out of cell; acts like a skin around the cell
   E L C L   E M B A R N M E _____

2. The brain of the cell; controls the cell's activities
   C L U S N U E _____

3. Gelatin-like substance with chemicals and water that contains other structures that perform cell functions P S A C T Y L O M _____

4. Receive direction from the DNA to make proteins
   S M O E I B R O S _____

5. Use food molecules to make and release energy
   C M A I I T R O D N H O _____

6. Move waste proteins from cell G L O I G   D B O I S E _____

7. Where a plant cell's food (sugar) is made
   H L C O R P S T A O L S _____

ACTIVITY 140   Cell Processes

Name:_____

Date:_____

Which process is happening in each situation?

osmosis	endocytosis	mitosis
exocytosis	active transport	diffusion

1. The nucleus of a cell divides into two so that two new cells can form.

   _____

2. Water is sucked up in the root of a plant. _____

3. Particles spread out to where there is more room. _____

4. Amoebas take in food by folding cell membranes to enclose larger particles.

   _____

5. Energy is used to move materials through a cell membrane. _____

6. Vacuoles fuse with their cell membrane and release their contents on the outside of the cell. _____

Life Sciences

ACTIVITY 141 Energy in Cells

Name:_____

Date:_____

Match each term with its description.

> photosynthesis   respiration   fermentation

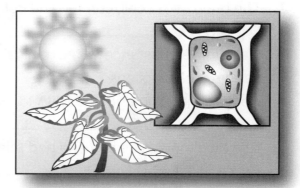

1. This process releases part of the energy from food molecules when there is no oxygen. _____

2. This process happens in plants containing chlorophyll when they change light energy into chemical energy. _____

3. This process is a series of chemical reactions that produce the final breakdown and release of energy from food. _____

ACTIVITY 142 Viruses

Name:_____

Date:_____

Circle the word in the parentheses that makes each sentence correct.

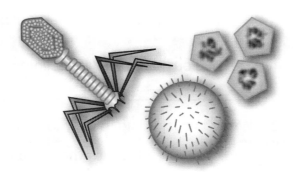

1. A virus is a structure that contains hereditary material and is surrounded by a (protein / cellular) covering.

2. Viruses reproduce only within (living / dead) host cells.

3. A(n) (latent / active) virus destroys its host cell.

4. A(n) (latent / active) virus may hide for many years before switching on.

5. Viruses cause (accelerated growth / diseases) in their hosts.

6. Some viral illnesses can be prevented with (antibiotics / vaccines).

Life Sciences

ACTIVITY 143 Binomial Nomenclature

Name:_____

Date:_____

Bionomial Nomenclature provides a scientific name for all living organisms. It consists of two terms in Latin. The first describes the genus and the second is the specific name.

Example: A domestic dog is called *Canis familiaris.*
A polar bear is called *Ursus maritimus.*
A housecat is called *Felis catus.*

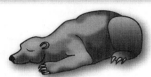

Shade the circle of the common name for each animal below.

1. *Ursus americanus* ⓐ a wolf ⓑ a black bear ⓒ a lion

2. *Canis latrans* ⓐ a brown bear ⓑ a lynx ⓒ a coyote

3. *Felis concolor* ⓐ a mountain lion ⓑ a condor ⓒ a horse

4. *Canis lupus* ⓐ a gray wolf ⓑ a lion ⓒ a leopard

5. *Ursus arctos* ⓐ brown bear ⓑ a Labrador ⓒ a cheetah

ACTIVITY 144 Classification Groups

Name:_____

Date:_____

Unscramble the names of these groups used in classification and number them in order from largest (broadest) to smallest (most specific).

a. _____ H L Y P M U   _____

b. _____ D R E O R   _____

c. _____ P I C S E S E   _____

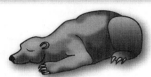

d. _____ D N G I K M O   _____

e. _____ M L Y I A F   _____

f. _____ S E G N U   _____

g. _____ S L C A S   _____

Life Sciences

ACTIVITY 145 The Kingdoms

Name:_____

Date:_____

In the chart, write the characteristics that fit the kingdoms.

Kingdom	Single or multi-celled? (or both)	Other characteristics
Monerans		
Protists		
Fungi		
Plants		
Animals		

Other Characteristics:

Cannot make own food

Mushrooms are in this kingdom

Ferns are in this kingdom

Have nucleus; lives in moist surroundings

Bacteria are in this kingdom

ACTIVITY 146 Bacteria

Name:_____

Date:_____

Write "T" for true or "F" for false.

1. _____ Bacteria usually reproduce by fission.

2. _____ All bacteria contain DNA.

3. _____ There are two types of bacteria: eubacteria and archaebacteria.

4. _____ Eubacteria exist in extreme conditions.

5. _____ All bacteria make their own food.

6. _____ Bacteria come in three basic shapes: spheres, rods, and spirals.

7. _____ All bacteria make humans sick.

8. _____ Many cheeses are made using bacteria.

Life Sciences

ACTIVITY 147 Protists

Name:_____

Date:_____

```
M F O G F U B Z N T L L Q D G
H H O Z G L J X I E U A C U M
Q J X S Q V A L G A E L L L M
D I N O F L A G E L L A T E S
E S M J T O P R E P N M H K D
U E M S A A V C R L H B L D T
G T H J D U X O W S L Y B V V
L A Y F Y O T X N M T A A R P
E I T I K O P W V S L B T E I
N L E L Z F R O M Q V I Z E D
O I I O S N A O Z O R O P S S
I C A A J W T S G I T P C T Y
D N N D K A U N M J H W Q L Y
S B R T I Y R I T I Q R G V Z
D M B D V I G B B F Y C W D E
```

Find these "protist" words in the word search.

ALGAE
DINOFLAGELLATES
CILIATES
DIATOMS
FLAGELLATES
PROTOZOANS
EUGLENOIDS
SPOROZOANS
RHIZOPODS

ACTIVITY 148 Fungi

Name:_____

Date:_____

Use the words from the box to fill in the blanks.

| chlorophyll | humid | saprophytes | walls |
| recyclers | celled | decompose | soil |

Fungi are sometimes called "nature's _____" because they

help to _____ organic materials. Most fungi are many-

_____. They have cell _____

and are anchored in _____. They grow best

in warm, _____ places. They do not contain

_____ and therefore cannot make their own food.

They are _____ because they feed on decaying or

dead tissues.

Life Sciences

ACTIVITY 149 **Seedless Plants**

Name:_____

Date:_____

Draw lines from each type of seedless plant to the
facts that are true about them. Facts will connect with more than one plant.

1. Bryophytes (liverworts and mosses)

2. Ground pines and spike mosses

3. Ferns

a. vascular plants

b. nonvascular plants

c. reproduce by spores

d. only a few cells thick

e. needle-like leaves

f. have stems and leaves

ACTIVITY 150 **Seed Plants**

Name:_____

Date:_____

List each plant type under the correct heading.

vegetables	palm tree	pine tree	spruce tree
cactus	grass	oak tree	cherry tree
fir tree	tulips	junipers	

Gymnosperms   Angiosperms

_____   _____

_____   _____

_____   _____

_____   _____

   _____

_____

Life Sciences

ACTIVITY 151   Animal or Not?

Name:_____

Date:_____

Circle the word in the parentheses that makes each sentence correct.

1. Animals (can / cannot) make their own food.

2. (Some / All) animals eat both plants and other animals.

3. Animals (digest / absorb) their food.

4. (Most / All) animals can move from one place to another.

5. Animals are made of (one type / many types) of cells.

6. Most animal cells are (prokaryotic / eukaryotic).

ACTIVITY 152   Vertebrates and Invertebrates

Name:_____

Date:_____

List each item under the correct heading to indicate if it is a vertebrate or an invertebrate.

snail	wasp	alligator	zebra	ant	snake
fly	duck	earthworm	turtle	frog	clam
cat	slug	spider	horse	human	sponge

Invertebrates   **Vertebrates**

_____   _____

_____   _____

_____   _____

_____   _____

_____   _____

_____   _____

_____   _____

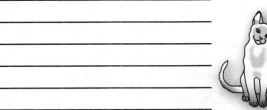

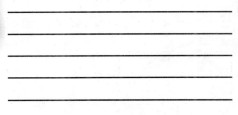

Life Sciences

ACTIVITY 153 Flatworms, Roundworms, Sponges, and Cnidarians

Name:_____

Date:_____

Which invertebrates are we?

| flatworms   roundworms   sponges   cnidarians |

1. We are the most simple of all animals.
   Our soft bodies have two layers of cells.
   We live in water and filter food from it.
   What are we? _____

2. We have soft, flattened bodies.
   We search for our food.
   Most of us are parasites.
   What are we? _____

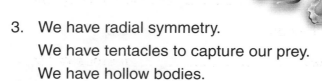

3. We have radial symmetry.
   We have tentacles to capture our prey.
   We have hollow bodies.
   What are we? _____

4. Our bodies are tube-like
   We are the most widespread
   animal on earth.
   What are we? _____

ACTIVITY 154 Mollusks

Name:_____

Date:_____

Use the descriptions to help you decide which type of mollusk each picture shows.

Gastropods have a single shell or no shell. They move by sliding on secreted mucus.
Bivalves have two shells that open and close. They are filter feeders.
Cephalopods generally have no shell. They have tentacles.

1. clams

_____

2. squid

_____

3. snail

_____

4. slug

_____

5. octopus

_____

6. scallop

_____

Life Sciences

ACTIVITY 155 Annelids

Name:_____

Date:_____

Use the words in the box to fill in the blanks.

leeches	soil	hundred
flexible	attach	earthworms
sections	suck	

Segmented worms have bodies with different

_____. This allows them to be

_____. One type of segmented worms are _____.

These annelids have more than one _____ segments. They travel

through the _____, eating it as they go.

_____ have flat bodies. They _____ themselves to

hosts, from which they _____ blood.

- -

ACTIVITY 156 Arthropods

Name:_____

Date:_____

Circle the two facts that are true about each type of arthropod.

1. Insects
    a. Have three pairs of legs.
    b. Have no antennae.
    c. Have three body sections.

2. Arachnids
    a. Have three body sections.
    b. Have no antennae.
    c. Have four pairs of legs.

3. Crustaceans
    a. Have a hard exoskeleton.
    b. Have gills.
    c. Have segmented bodies.

4. Millipedes and
    Centipedes
    a. Have a hard exoskeleton.
    b. Have one pair of antennae.
    c. Have segmented bodies.

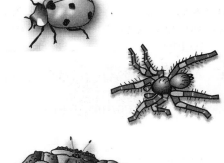

Life Sciences

ACTIVITY 157) Insects

Name:_____

Date:_____

Fill in the blanks with the correct numbers and then use the information to help you decide if each organism is an insect or not. Write yes or no under each picture.

Insects have: _____ pairs of legs.
_____ body sections.
_____ pair of antennae.
_____ or _____ pair of wings (sometimes)

1. fly

_____

2. tick

_____

3. bee

_____

4. mosquito

_____

5. louse

_____

6. lobster

_____

7. scorpion

_____

8. ant

_____

9. butterfly

_____

ACTIVITY 158) Arachnids

Name:_____

Date:_____

1. Name the two body regions of an arachnid.

_____ and _____

2. All arachnids have _____ pairs of legs, which are attached

   to the _____ (body region).

3. Arachnids have (0 / 1 / 2) pair of antennae.

4. The most common arachnids are

   _____.

5. All arachnids have 6 eyes.   True / False

6. There are over (2,000 / 60,000) species of spiders.

Life Sciences

ACTIVITY 159   Crustaceans and Echinoderms

Name: _____

Date: _____

Beside each picture, write "C" if it is a crustacean or "E" if it is an echinoderm.

1. sea star   _____

2. crab   _____

3. sea urchin   _____

4. sand dollar   _____

5. lobster   _____

6. shrimp   _____

ACTIVITY 160   Vertebrates

Name: _____

Date: _____

Fill in the chart with the indicated information.

Group of Vertebrates	Endothermic or Ectothermic?	Two Characteristics	Two Examples
		- Have scales and fins - Live in water	
Amphibians			
Reptiles			
		- Lay eggs with hard shells -	- robin -
Mammals			- tiger -

Life Sciences

ACTIVITY 161   Animal Adaptations/ Bird Beaks and Feet

Name:_____

Date:_____

Match each bird adaptation to its purpose.

1. _____ webbed feet   a. wading
2. _____ sharp, hooked beaks   b. drilling for insects
3. _____ long, thin beaks   c. spearing fish
4. _____ three toes forward–one back   d. perching
5. _____ two toes forward–two back   e. swimming
6. _____ spear-shaped beak   f. scooping up fish
7. _____ spoon-shaped beaks   g. catching and tearing prey
8. _____ very long, skinny legs   h. climbing

ACTIVITY 162   Invertebrates and Vertebrates Review/Test Practice

Name:_____

Date:_____

Shade in the circle of the correct answer.

1. Which organism has two body regions?
   - (a.) annelid
   - (b.) arachnid
   - (c.) cnidarian

2. Which of these organisms is endothermic?
   - (a.) mammal
   - (b.) insect
   - (c.) mollusk

3. Which vertebrates have dry, scaly skin?
   - (a.) amphibians
   - (b.) birds
   - (c.) reptiles

4. Which invertebrates develop through metamorphosis?
   - (a.) arthropods
   - (b.) echinoderms
   - (c.) cnidarians

5. Which of these organisms is a parasite?
   - (a.) tapeworm
   - (b.) segmented worm
   - (c.) sponge

6. Which arthropods have exoskeletons?
   - (a.) only crustaceans
   - (b.) all of them
   - (c.) crustaceans and insects

The Periodic Table of Elements

Metals — Transition Metals — Nonmetals

Key:
- Atomic Number
- Atomic Symbol
- Element Name
- Atomic Mass (most stable isotope of radioactive elements in parentheses)

Example: 1 H Hydrogen 1.0079

1 H Hydrogen 1.0079																	2 He Helium 4.003
3 Li Lithium 6.941	4 Be Beryllium 9.012											5 B Boron 10.811	6 C Carbon 12.011	7 N Nitrogen 14.007	8 O Oxygen 15.999	9 F Fluorine 18.998	10 Ne Neon 20.180
11 Na Sodium 22.990	12 Mg Magnesium 24.305											13 Al Aluminum 26.982	14 Si Silicon 28.086	15 P Phosphorus 30.974	16 S Sulfur 32.065	17 Cl Chlorine 35.453	18 Ar Argon 39.948
19 K Potassium 39.098	20 Ca Calcium 40.08	21 Sc Scandium 44.956	22 Ti Titanium 47.867	23 V Vanadium 50.942	24 Cr Chromium 51.996	25 Mn Manganese 54.938	26 Fe Iron 55.845	27 Co Cobalt 58.933	28 Ni Nickel 58.69	29 Cu Copper 63.546	30 Zn Zinc 65.409	31 Ga Gallium 69.723	32 Ge Germanium 72.64	33 As Arsenic 74.922	34 Se Selenium 78.96	35 Br Bromine 79.904	36 Kr Krypton 83.80
37 Rb Rubidium 85.47	38 Sr Strontium 87.62	39 Y Yttrium 88.906	40 Zr Zirconium 91.224	41 Nb Niobium 92.906	42 Mo Molybdenum 95.94	43 Tc Technetium (98)	44 Ru Ruthenium 101.07	45 Rh Rhodium 102.91	46 Pd Palladium 106.42	47 Ag Silver 107.87	48 Cd Cadmium 112.41	49 In Indium 114.82	50 Sn Tin 118.71	51 Sb Antimony 121.76	52 Te Tellurium 127.60	53 I Iodine 126.90	54 Xe Xenon 131.29
55 Cs Cesium 132.90	56 Ba Barium 137.33	♦ 57-71 Lanthanide series (rare earth elements)	72 Hf Hafnium 178.49	73 Ta Tantalum 180.95	74 W Tungsten 183.84	75 Re Rhenium 186.21	76 Os Osmium 190.23	77 Ir Iridium 192.22	78 Pt Platinum 195.08	79 Au Gold 196.97	80 Hg Mercury 200.59	81 Tl Thallium 204.38	82 Pb Lead 207.2	83 Bi Bismuth 208.98	84 Po Polonium (209)	85 At Astatine (210)	86 Rn Radon (222)
87 Fr Francium (223)	88 Ra Radium (226)	◊ 89-103 Actinide series (radioactive earth elements)	104 Rf Rutherfordium (261)	105 Db Dubnium (262)	106 Sg Seaborgium (266)	107 Bh Bohrium (264)	108 Hs Hassium (277)	109 Mt Meitnerium (268)	110 Ds Darmstadtium (281)	111 Rg Roentgenium (272)	112 Uub Ununbium (285)	113 Uut Ununtrium (284)	114 Uuq Ununquadium (289)	115 Uup Ununpentium (288)	116 Uuh Ununhexium (292)	117 Uus Ununseptium (294)	118 Uuo Ununoctium (294)

♦	57 La Lanthanum 138.91	58 Ce Cerium 140.12	59 Pr Praseodymium 140.91	60 Nd Neodymium 144.24	61 Pm Promethium (145)	62 Sm Samarium 150.36	63 Eu Europium 151.96	64 Gd Gadolinium 157.25	65 Tb Terbium 158.92	66 Dy Dysprosium 162.50	67 Ho Holmium 164.93	68 Er Erbium 167.26	69 Tm Thulium 168.93	70 Yb Ytterbium 173.04	71 Lu Lutetium 174.97
◊	89 Ac Actinium (227)	90 Th Thorium 232.04	91 Pa Protactinium 231.04	92 U Uranium 238.03	93 Np Neptunium (237)	94 Pu Plutonium (244)	95 Am Americium (243)	96 Cm Curium (247)	97 Bk Berkelium (247)	98 Cf Californium (251)	99 Es Einsteinium (252)	100 Fm Fermium (257)	101 Md Mendelevium (258)	102 No Nobelium (259)	103 Lr Lawrencium (262)

Answer Keys

Activity 1 (p. 2)
1. h   2. c   3. m   4. a   5. k
6. e   7. o   8. b   9. j   10. d
11. f   12. g   13. n   14. i   15. l

Activity 2 (p. 2)
1. Life   2. Earth and Space
3. Physical   4. Life
5. Social   6. Mathematics
7. Life   8. Earth and Space
9. Earth and Space/Physical   10. Physical
11. Mathematics   12. Life
13. Earth and Space   14. Social
15. Earth and Space   16. Life
17. Social   18. Mathematics
19. Life   20. Life

Activity 3 (p. 3)
1. T   2. T   3. F   4. T
5. F   6. F   7. T   8. T

Activity 4 (p. 3)
Mass: kilogram   kg
Volume: cubic meter   m³
Time: second   s
Temperature: kelvin   K
Length: meter   m

Activity 5 (p. 4)
1. mass   2. same   3. weight, gravity
4. Temperature, Kelvin, absolute, boils   5. time

Activity 6 (p. 4)
1. A   2. C
3. The mass is the same in all three.
4. The volume is largest in C, the biggest square.
5. iron

Activity 7 (p. 5)
These words should be circled: paper, milk, steel, peach, skin, glue, rock, book, rose, planet, mud, hair, water, leaf, spit, pencil, blood, diamond, tape, sand, germs, tree, nest

Activity 8 (p. 5)
1. atom   2. nucleus   3. proton
4. electron   5. neutron   6. atomic number
7. isotopes   8. electron cloud

Activity 9 (p. 6)
1. atoms   2. constant, random   3. higher
4. less   5. melting point, liquid   6. Crystalline

Activity 10 (p. 6)
1. c   2. b   3. c   4. a   5. a

Activity 11 (p. 7)
Make these changes:
common to rare or uncommon
solid to gas
protons to electrons
trees to atmosphere
Western to Northern
moon to stars or sun

Activity 12 (p. 7)
Answers will vary. Should describe shape, color, size, texture, etc.

Activity 13 (p. 8)
1. c   2. a   3. e   4. b   5. d

Activity 14 (p. 8)
1. aluminum   2. hydrogen
3. cobalt   4. oxygen
5. titanium   6. helium
7. carbon   8. radon
9. lithium   10. sodium
11. iron   12. potassium
13. platinum   14. copper
15. sulfur   16. nitrogen
17. iodine   18. silicon
19. nickel   20. mercury
21. magnesium   22. calcium
23. neon   24. plutonium

Activity 15 (p. 9)

Lithium:	Li	3	6.941	metal
Iron:	Fe	26	55.845	metal
Arsenic:	As	33	74.922	metalloid
Helium:	He	2	4.003	nonmetal
Titanium:	Ti	22	47.867	metal
Silicon:	Si	14	28.086	metalloid
Radon:	Rn	86	(222)	nonmetal

Activity 16 (p. 9)
1. T   2. T   3. F   4. T   5. T
6. F   7. F   8. T   9. F   10. F

Activity 17 (p. 10)
1. carbon   2. iron   3. aluminum
4. hydrogen   5. arsenic   6. mercury
7. silicon

Activity 18 (p. 10)
Statements 1, 2, and 6 go under "compounds"
Statements 3, 4, and 5 go under "mixtures"

Activity 19 (p. 11)
1. silver   2. nickel   3. 2 mL   4. 3.24

Activity 20 (p. 11)
1. P   2. C   3. C   4. C
5. P   6. P   7. P   8. P
9. C   10. P   11. C   12. P

Activity 21 (p. 12)
solution, dissolves, solute, solvent, Gaseous, Liquid, water, soda pop, Solid, alloys

Activity 22 (p. 12)
1. Because so many solutes can dissolve in it.
2. A saturated solution is one where no more solute can dissolve in it in the condition it is in. An unsaturated solution has room for more solute.
3. A concentrated solution has a large amount of solute. A dilute solution contains a small amount of solute.
4. Temperature (heat it up)

Activity 23 (p. 13)
1. T   2. T   3. F   4. F   5. T
6. T   7. T   8. T   9. T   10. T

Activity 24 (p. 13)
1. neutral
2. somewhat acidic
3. somewhat basic
4. extremely acidic
5. somewhat basic
6. extremely acidic
7. extremely basic
8. somewhat acidic
9. somewhat basic

Activity 25 (p. 14)
1. 1 atom of carbon
   2 atoms of oxygen
2. 1 atom of nitrogen
   3 atoms of hydrogen
3. 1 atom of lead
   1 atom of sulfur
   3 atoms of oxygen

Activity 26 (p. 14)
constant, inverse, pressure, increase, volume, decrease

Activity 27 (p. 15)
1. d   2. g   3. f   4. a
5. b   6. c   7. e

Activity 28 (p. 15)
1. If an object's density is less than that of the fluid, it will float in the fluid. If its density is greater than that of the fluid, it will sink in the fluid.
2. displaced, weight

Activity 29 (p. 16)

Activity 30 (p. 16)
1. kinetic   2. all motion stops

Fahrenheit:	32°	212°	-459°
Celsius:	0°	100°	-273°
Kelvin:	273°	373°	0°

Activity 31 (p. 17)

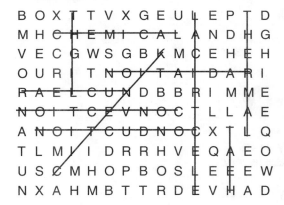

Activity 32 (p. 17)
1. transfer   2. kinetic   3. thermal energy
4. Heat   5. conduction   6. convection
7. radiation

Activity 33 (p. 18)
1. C   2. I   3. I   4. I
5. C   6. C   7. I   8. C

Activity 34 (p. 18)
1. Any three of these: food, oil, gas, coal
2. Exothermic reactions release energy. Endothermic reactions absorb energy.
3. Answers will vary. Possiblities include stirring, changing the temperature, adding a catalyst.

Activity 35 (p. 19)
1. a   2. a   3. c   4. b   5. a

Activity 36 (p. 19)
1. 56 miles   2. 5.25 km   3. 8:30

Activity 37 (p. 20)
1. T   2. T   3. F   4. T
5. F   6. T   7. T   8. T

Activity 38 (p. 20)
1. the earth   2. different things   3. but not
4. changes   5. Mass   6. does not
7. remains the same

Activity 39 (p. 21)

Grams	Kilograms	Pounds
100	0.1	0.22
3,500	3.5	7.7
2,700	2.7	5.94
7,500	7.5	16.5
500	0.5	1.1
9,000	9	19.8
6,000	6	13.2
2,000	2	4.4
300	0.3	0.66
10,000	10	22

Activity 40 (p. 21)
1. a   2. c   3. b

Activity 41 (p. 22)
Answers will vary.

Activity 42 (p. 22)
1. g   2. h   3. c   4. b   5. f
6. i   7. a   8. d   9. e

Activity 43 (p. 23)
balanced, normal, right, resistance, terminal, accelerate, speed up, slow down, turn

Activity 44 (p. 23)
1. 96
2. A player who weighs 102 kg running at 5 meters/sec.
3. 6 meters/sec

Activity 45 (p. 24)
1. work   2. positive   3. negative
4. joules   5. power   6. watts

Activity 46 (p. 24)
1. wedge   2. screw   3. wheel and axle
4. inclined plane   5. wedge   6. lever
7. wheel and axle   8. lever, wheel and axle
9. pulley

Activity 47 (p. 25)
1. simple   2. compound   3. effort force
4. resistance force   5. Mechanical advantage
6. efficiency

Activity 48 (p. 25)
vibrations, energy, matter, Mechanical, liquid, transferred, Sound, Electromagnetic, magnetic, Light

Activity 49 (p. 26)
1. c   2. d   3. b   4. a

Activity 50 (p. 26)
Change: acute to right, mechanical to electromagnetic, opposite to same, matter to energy, transverse to compressional, tips to crests, dips to troughs,

Activity 51 (p. 27)
1. radio   2. gamma rays   3. hertz   4. 96

Activity 52 (p. 27)
1. T   2. F   3. T   4. T
5. T   6. T   7. F   8. T

Activity 53 (p. 28)
1. Reflection - b   2. Refraction - d
3. Diffraction - e   4. Interference - g

Activity 54 (p. 28)
1. b   2. c   3. b   4. a   5. a

Activity 55 (p. 29)
1. Light waves spread out in all directions from the source.
2. Opaque materials don't allow any light to pass through them.
3. Transparent materials allow almost all light to pass through them.
4. Translucent materials only allow some light to pass through them.

Activity 56 (p. 29)
1. narrow   2. longest   3. reflected
4. white   5. black   6. all

Activity 57 (p. 30)

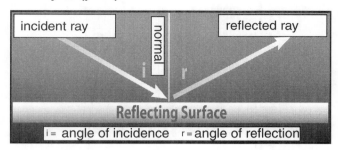

incident ray | normal | reflected ray
i | r
Reflecting Surface
i = angle of incidence   r = angle of reflection

Activity 58 (p. 30)
Answers will vary. Possibilities include:

Very smooth surfaces cause parallel light rays to be reflected in a single direction, producing a sharp image. Rough or uneven surfaces cause light rays to be reflected in many different directions.

Activity 59 (p. 31)
A. concave   B. plane   C. convex

Activity 60 (p. 31)
space, medium, atoms, boundary, speed, bends, refraction

Activity 61 (p. 32)
1. proton   2. electron   3. neutron

Activity 62 (p. 32)
electrons, neutral, added, positively, negatively, move, nucleus

Activity 63 (p. 33)
1. I   2. I   3. C   4. I   5. C
6. C   7. I   8. C   9. I   10. C

Activity 64 (p. 33)
a. 4   b. 3   c. 6   d. 1   e. 5   f. 2

Activity 65 (p. 34)
1. F change sudden burst to continuous flow
2. T   3. T   4. T
5. F change mixed together to kept separate
6. T   7. T
8. F change positive charges to electrical potential

Activity 66 (p. 34)
1. voltage   2. amperes   3. watts
4. 80 watts   5. 600 watts   6. 960 watts

Activity 67 (p. 35)
1. b   2. d   3. e

Activity 68 (p. 35)
1. amperes   2. watts   3. volts
4. ohms   5. 120 volts 6. 9.375 ohms
7. 12 amperes

Activity 69 (p. 36)
1. A, C   2. B   3. D

Activity 70 (p. 36)
1. 0.83 amps   2. washing machine
3. 13.33 amps 4. 12.5 amps 5. floor fan

Activity 71 (p. 37)
1. poles   2. cannot   3. repel
4. magnetic domain   5. is   6. magnetic field

Activity 72 (p. 37)
Answers will vary. Possibilities include:

When the north pole of the bar magnet is held close to the first paper clip, each magnetic domain in the paper clip lines up with the magnet, and the top of the paper clip becomes a south pole of a new magnet, thus attracting the next paper clip in the chain.

Activity 73 (p. 38)
Statements 1, 2, 4, and 5 should be circled.

Activity 74 (p. 38)
1. a   2. c   3. b   4. b   5. a   6. c

Activity 75 (p. 39)
1. All minerals are formed by natural processes.
2. All minerals are inorganic, or not alive.
3. Atoms in minerals are arranged in repeating patterns.
4. Every mineral has a definite chemical composition.

Activity 76 (p. 39)

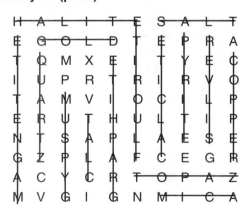

Activity 77 (p. 40)
Answers will vary. Possibilities include:
 When magma cools, its atoms come close together and combine to form compounds.
 When minerals are dissolved in liquids and the liquid evaporates, ions may join together to form crystals.

Activity 78 (p. 40)
 1. c   2. e   3. a   4. b   5. d

Activity 79 (p. 41)
 1. 2.5   2. 5.5   3. 4.5   4. diamond

Activity 80 (p. 41)
oxygen, silicon (or these two reversed), abundant, crust, building, silicates

Activity 81 (p. 42)
Igneous: a, j
Sedimentary: e, b, g, i
Metamorphic: c, d, f, h

Activity 82 (p. 42)
 1. compaction   2. weathering and erosion
 3. cementation

Activity 83 (p. 43)
environment, sediment, Mechanical, chemical, characteristics, weathering, oxidation

Activity 84 (p. 43)
 1. leaves   2. twigs   3. insects
 4. water   5. rock   6. air
 7. minerals   8. worms   9. algae
 10. fungi

Activity 85 (p. 44)
 1. mass movement   2. rockslide
 3. slump   4. mudflows   5. creep

Activity 86 (p. 44)
 1. T   2. F   3. T   4. T
 5. F   6. T   7. T

Activity 87 (p. 45)

Activity 88 (p. 45)
 1. stream erosion   2. rill erosion
 3. sheet erosion   4. gully erosion

Activity 89 (p. 46)
 1. Water that soaks into the ground, collecting in spaces between rocks and soil
 2. Permeable rock allows water to seep through it. Impermeable rock does not.
 3. A layer of permeable rock underground through which water can move
 4. The top layer of the zone of saturation underground in rocks (filled with water)

Activity 90 (p. 46)
 1. heated   2. steam   3. limestone
 4. calcite   5. dissolved

Activity 91 (p. 47)
Under renewable resources: solar energy, wind, hydroelectric power, geothermal energy
Under nonrenewable resources: coal, natural gas, oil

Activity 92 (p. 47)
 1. b   2. a   3. c   4. c   5. a   6. b

Activity 93 (p. 48)
The circle graph should show chloride 55%, sodium 30.6%, sulfate 7.7%, magnesium 3.7%, calcium 1.2%, potassium 1.1%, and other salts 0.7%

Activity 94 (p. 48)
energy, particles, crest, trough, wind, tides, gravity, moon

Activity 95 (p. 49)
 1. c   2. d   3. a   4. e   5. b

Activity 96 (p. 49)
 1. tension   2. compression   3. shear

Activity 97 (p. 50)

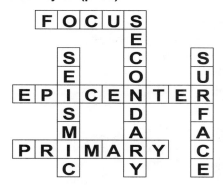

Activity 98 (p. 50)
seismologists, magnitude, seismograph, Richter, energy, seismic

Activity 99 (p. 51)
1. The name given to the supposed single landmass made up of all the current continents connected together at some point many years ago.
2. That the continents have slowly drifted apart over many years to their current locations

Activity 100 (p. 51)
spreading, molten, mid-ocean, erupts, older, continuously, sea floor

Activity 101 (p. 52)
1. Eurasian   2. Antarctic   3. Pacific
4. Nazca   5. Caribbean   6. African
7. North American 8. South American
9. Indo Australian

Activity 102 (p. 52)
1. divergent boundary   2. convergent boundary
3. transform boundary   4. transform boundary
5. divergent boundary   6. convergent boundary

Activity 103 (p. 53)
Answers will vary. Possibilities include:
Most volcanoes lie along plate boundaries.
Many islands are/have active volcanoes.
Most volcanoes are in the Pacific "Ring of Fire."

Activity 104 (p. 53)
1. magma   2. side vent
3. lava   4. vent
5. crater   6. pipe
7. magma chamber

Activity 105 (p. 54)
1. T   2. T   3. F   4. T
5. T   6. F   7. T   8. T

Activity 106 (p. 54)
1. c   2. e   3. b   4. a   5. d   6. f

Activity 107 (p. 55)
1. troposphere   2. stratosphere   3. mesosphere
4. ionosphere   5. mesosphere   6. ionosphere
7. stratosphere   8. thermosphere   9. exosphere
10. troposphere

Activity 108 (p. 55)
1. nitrogen   2. oxygen, ozone
3. argon, carbon dioxide   4. water vapor
5. dust, smoke, salt, chemicals

Activity 109 (p. 56)
1. T   2. F   3. T   4. T
5. F   6. F   7. T   8. F

Activity 110 (p. 56)
1. the sun   2. electromagnetic
3. infrared and ultraviolet 4. scattering
5. greenhouse

Activity 111 (p. 57)
1. conduction   2. closer together   3. Convection
4. Convection   5. sinks, rises

Activity 112 (p. 57)
1. Winds occur when cool air meets warm air.
2. Surface winds are caused by differences in air pressure.
3. Unequal heating causes differences in air pressure in the atmosphere.
4. An anemometer is used to measure wind speed.
5. Narrow belts of strong winds at high altitudes are called jet streams.

Activity 113 (p. 58)
energy, tropical, polar, spinning, shifted, opposite, Coriolis, patterns

Activity 114 (p. 58)
1. Polar Easterlies   2. Prevailing Westerlies
3. Northeast Trade Winds   4. Doldrums
5. Southeast Trade Winds   6. Prevailing Westerlies
7. Polar Easterlies

Activity 115 (p. 59)
1. e   2. d   3. g   4. f
5. b   6. c   7. a

Activity 116 (p. 59)
a. 3   b. 5   c. 1   d. 6   e. 2   f. 4

Activity 117 (p. 60)
1. stratus   2. cumulus   3. cirrus
4. nimbus   5. fog

Activity 118 (p. 60)
Precipitation: any form of water falling from the clouds
1. c   2. b   3. d   4. a   5. f   6. e

Activity 119 (p. 61)
1. continental   2. maritime
3. tropical   4. polar

Activity 120 (p. 61)
1. cold; if humid - heavy rain, if dry - cloudy skies
2. warm; varied weather - scattered clouds if dry, showers and light rain or fog if humid
3. stationary; extended periods of clouds and precipitation
4. occluded; cloudy and rainy or snowy

Activity 121 (p. 62)
1. thunderstorm   2. hurricane   3. tornado

Activity 122 (p. 62)
1. T   2. T   3. T   4. F
5. T   6. F   7. F   8. T

Activity 123 (p. 63)
1. front   2. northeast   3. minutes
4. Alley   5. heavier   6. Doppler

Activity 124 (p. 63)
1. Atlantic   2. Pacific   3. Indian
a. 4   b. 2   c. 3   d. 1

Activity 125 (p. 64)
1. humidity, air pressure, temperature
2. any of these: weather balloons, weather stations, satellites, radar, local observers, computers, National Weather Service, etc.
3. c   4. d   5. a   6. e   7. b

Activity 126 (p. 64)
1. any of these: fronts, temperature, precipitation, cloud cover, wind speed, lightning strikes, water vapor, hurricanes, etc.
2. cold   3. warm   4. stationary   5. occluded
6. fog   7. hail   8. rain   9. snow
10. sleet

Activity 127 (p. 65)
1. polar, temperate, tropical
2. temperate, tropical
3. temperate, tropical
4. polar, temperate, tropical
5. temperate, tropical
6. temperate, polar
7. polar

Activity 128 (p. 65)
1. polar   2. polar   3. dry
4. temperate marine   5. dry
6. temperate continental   7. tropical
8. temperate marine   9. tropical
10. temperate marine   11. temperate continental

Activity 129 (p. 66)
greenhouse, heating, gases, carbon dioxide, sun, surface, prevents, Global warming, temperatures, increase

Activity 130 (p. 66)
1. Such an eruption sends enormous volumes of dust and ash into the air. It then blocks much solar radiation, and the planet cools.
2. If continents shift locations, they move into areas where they receive different amounts of solar radiation and have different wind and weather patterns.
3. If the sun emits more or less radiation, then the temperatures will be altered correspondingly.

Activity 131 (p. 67)
1. day and night; seasons
2. It is directly above the equator, and day and night hours will be equal.
3. As the moon revolves around the earth, you see different portions of its lighted side.
4. It reflects sunlight from its surface.

Activity 132 (p. 67)
1. New moon   2. Waxing crescent
3. First quarter   4. Waxing gibbous
5. Full Moon   6. Waning gibbous
7. Third quarter   8. Waning Crescent

Activity 133 (p. 68)
1. T   2. F   3. T   4. T   5. T
6. T   7. F   8. T   9. F   10. F

Activity 134 (p. 68)
1. b   2. c   3. a   4. a   5. c   6. a

Activity 135 (p. 69)

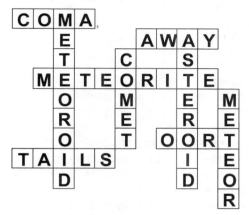

Activity 136 (p. 69)
1. bluish-white, yellow, reddish-orange
2. T   3. F   4. T   5. F   6. T
7. A large cloud of dust and gas, parts of which can eventually form into a sun

Activity 137 (p. 70)
1. a. photosphere   b. chromosphere
   c. core   d. prominence
   e. sunspot   f. corona
2. corona   3. photosphere   4. core
5. sunspots   6. prominences

Activity 138 (p. 70)
stars, gravitational, Spiral, core, Milky Way, Elliptical, enormous, Irregular, shapes

Activity 139 (p. 71)
1. cell membrane   2. nucleus
3. cytoplasm   4. ribosomes
5. mitochondria   6. Golgi bodies
7. chloroplasts

Activity 140 (p. 71)
1. mitosis   2. osmosis   3. diffusion
4. endocytosis 5. active transport 6. exocytosis

Activity 141 (p. 72)
1. fermentation   2. photosynthesis
3. respiration

Activity 142 (p. 72)
1. protein   2. living   3. active
4. latent   5. diseases   6. vaccines

Activity 143 (p. 73)
1. b   2. c   3. a   4. a   5. a

Activity 144 (p. 73)
a. 2; phylum   b. 4; order   c. 7; species
d. 1; kingdom   e. 5; family   f. 6; genus
g. 3; class

Activity 145 (p. 74)

Monerans:	Single	Bacteria are in this kingdom
Protists:	Both	Have nucleus; live in moist surroundings
Fungi:	Both	Mushrooms are in this kingdom
Plants:	Multi-celled	Ferns are in this kingdom
Animals:	Multi-celled	Cannot make own food

Activity 146 (p. 74)
1. T   2. T   3. T   4. F
5. F   6. T   7. F   8. T

Activity 147 (p. 75)

Activity 148 (p. 75)
recyclers, decompose, celled, walls, soil, humid, chlorophyll, saprophytes

Activity 149 (p. 76)
1. b, c, and d   2. a, c, and e
3. a, c, and f

Activity 150 (p. 76)
Under gymnosperms: pine tree, spruce tree, fir tree, junipers
Under angiosperms: vegetables, palm tree, cactus, grass, oak tree, cherry tree, tulips

Activity 151 (p. 77)
1. cannot   2. Some   3. digest
4. Most   5. many types   6. eukaryotic

Activity 152 (p. 77)
Invertebrates: ant, clam, earthworm, fly, slug, snail,
    spider, sponge, wasp
Vertebrates: alligator, cat, duck, frog, horse, human,
    snake, turtle, zebra

Activity 153 (p. 78)
1. sponges   2. flatworms
3. cnidarians   4. roundworms

Activity 154 (p. 78)
1. bivalve   2. cephalopod   3. gastropod
4. gastropod   5. cephalopod   6. bivalve

Activity 155 (p. 79)
sections, flexible, earthworms, hundred, soil, Leeches,
attach, suck

Activity 156 (p. 79)
1. a, c   2. b, c   3. a, b   4. b, c

Activity 157 (p. 80)
3, 3, 1, 1, 2
1. yes   2. no   3. yes   4. yes
5. yes   6. no   7. no   8. yes
9. yes

Activity 158 (p. 80)
1. cephalothorax, abdomen
2. 4, cephalothorax
3. 0
4. spiders
5. False
6. 60,000

Activity 159 (p. 81)
1. E   2. C
3. E   4. E
5. C   6. C

Activity 160 (p. 81)
Fish: Ectothermic
             Have scales and fins; Live in water
             Trout, sharks, stingrays, salmon, etc.
Amphibians: Ectothermic
             Wet, slimy skin; Soft toes
             Larvae in water; Adults on land
             Frogs, toads, salamanders, newts, etc.
Reptiles: Ectothermic
             Dry, scaly skin; Lay leathery eggs
             Snake, lizard, turtle, alligator, crocodile, etc.
Birds: Endothermic
             Have feathers; Lay eggs with hard shells
             Robin, sparrow, eagle, etc.
Mammals: Endothermic
             Drink milk from mothers; Have hair or fur
             Tiger, cat, dog, horse, zebra, mouse, etc.

Activity 161 (p. 82)
1. e   2. g   3. b   4. d
5. h   6. c   7. f   8. a

Activity 162 (p. 82)
1. b   2. a   3. c   4. a   5. a   6. b